═══ MADE EASY PRESS ═══

2024 • 2025
Monthly
Budget
Planner

Two-Year Schedule Organizer with Financial Goals, Budget Planning, and Debt Tracker to Stay on Top of Your Money

Producer & International Distributor
eBookPro Publishing
www.ebook-pro.com

2024-2025 Monthly Budget Planner:

Two-Year Schedule Organizer with Financial Goals, Budget Planning, and Debt Tracker to Stay on Top of Your Money

Made Easy Press

Copyright © 2023 Made Easy Press

All rights reserved; No parts of this book may be reproduced or transmitted in any form or by any means, electronic or mechanical, including photocopying, recording, taping, or by any information retrieval system, without the permission, in writing, of the author.

Contact: agency@ebook-pro.com
ISBN 9789655753936

2024

January

su	mo	tu	we	th	fr	sa
	1	2	3	4	5	6
7	8	9	10	11	12	13
14	15	16	17	18	19	20
21	22	23	24	25	26	27
28	29	30	31			

February

su	mo	tu	we	th	fr	sa
				1	2	3
4	5	6	7	8	9	10
11	12	13	14	15	16	17
18	19	20	21	22	23	24
25	26	27	28	29		

March

su	mo	tu	we	th	fr	sa
					1	2
3	4	5	6	7	8	9
10	11	12	13	14	15	16
17	18	19	20	21	22	23
24	25	26	27	28	29	30
31						

April

su	mo	tu	we	th	fr	sa
	1	2	3	4	5	6
7	8	9	10	11	12	13
14	15	16	17	18	19	20
21	22	23	24	25	26	27
28	29	30				

May

su	mo	tu	we	th	fr	sa
			1	2	3	4
5	6	7	8	9	10	11
12	13	14	15	16	17	18
19	20	21	22	23	24	25
26	27	28	29	30	31	

June

su	mo	tu	we	th	fr	sa
						1
2	3	4	5	6	7	8
9	10	11	12	13	14	15
16	17	18	19	20	21	22
23	24	25	26	27	28	29
30						

July

su	mo	tu	we	th	fr	sa
	1	2	3	4	5	6
7	8	9	10	11	12	13
14	15	16	17	18	19	20
21	22	23	24	25	26	27
28	29	30	31			

August

su	mo	tu	we	th	fr	sa
				1	2	3
4	5	6	7	8	9	10
11	12	13	14	15	16	17
18	19	20	21	22	23	24
25	26	27	28	29	30	31

September

su	mo	tu	we	th	fr	sa
1	2	3	4	5	6	7
8	9	10	11	12	13	14
15	16	17	18	19	20	21
22	23	24	25	26	27	28
29	30					

October

su	mo	tu	we	th	fr	sa
		1	2	3	4	5
6	7	8	9	10	11	12
13	14	15	16	17	18	19
20	21	22	23	24	25	26
27	28	29	30	31		

November

su	mo	tu	we	th	fr	sa
					1	2
3	4	5	6	7	8	9
10	11	12	13	14	15	16
17	18	19	20	21	22	23
24	25	26	27	28	29	30

December

su	mo	tu	we	th	fr	sa
1	2	3	4	5	6	7
8	9	10	11	12	13	14
15	16	17	18	19	20	21
22	23	24	25	26	27	28
29	30	31				

2025

January

su	mo	tu	we	th	fr	sa
			1	2	3	4
5	6	7	8	9	10	11
12	13	14	15	16	17	18
19	20	21	22	23	24	25
26	27	28	29	30	31	

February

su	mo	tu	we	th	fr	sa
						1
2	3	4	5	6	7	8
9	10	11	12	13	14	15
16	17	18	19	20	21	22
23	24	25	26	27	28	

March

su	mo	tu	we	th	fr	sa
						1
2	3	4	5	6	7	8
9	10	11	12	13	14	15
16	17	18	19	20	21	22
23	24	25	26	27	28	29
30	31					

April

su	mo	tu	we	th	fr	sa
		1	2	3	4	5
6	7	8	9	10	11	12
13	14	15	16	17	18	19
20	21	22	23	24	25	26
27	28	29	30			

May

su	mo	tu	we	th	fr	sa
				1	2	3
4	5	6	7	8	9	10
11	12	13	14	15	16	17
18	19	20	21	22	23	24
25	26	27	28	29	30	31

June

su	mo	tu	we	th	fr	sa
1	2	3	4	5	6	7
8	9	10	11	12	13	14
15	16	17	18	19	20	21
22	23	24	25	26	27	28
29	30					

July

su	mo	tu	we	th	fr	sa
		1	2	3	4	5
6	7	8	9	10	11	12
13	14	15	16	17	18	19
20	21	22	23	24	25	26
27	28	29	30	31		

August

su	mo	tu	we	th	fr	sa
					1	2
3	4	5	6	7	8	9
10	11	12	13	14	15	16
17	18	19	20	21	22	23
24	25	26	27	28	29	30
31						

September

su	mo	tu	we	th	fr	sa
	1	2	3	4	5	6
7	8	9	10	11	12	13
14	15	16	17	18	19	20
21	22	23	24	25	26	27
28	29	30				

October

su	mo	tu	we	th	fr	sa
			1	2	3	4
5	6	7	8	9	10	11
12	13	14	15	16	17	18
19	20	21	22	23	24	25
26	27	28	29	30	31	

November

su	mo	tu	we	th	fr	sa
						1
2	3	4	5	6	7	8
9	10	11	12	13	14	15
16	17	18	19	20	21	22
23	24	25	26	27	28	29
30						

December

su	mo	tu	we	th	fr	sa
	1	2	3	4	5	6
7	8	9	10	11	12	13
14	15	16	17	18	19	20
21	22	23	24	25	26	27
28	29	30	31			

Birthday Log

January

February

March

April

May

June

Birthday Log

July

August

September

October

November

December

My 2024 Resolutions

1. ....
2. ....
3. ....
4. ....
5. ....
6. ....
7. ....
8. ....
9. ....
10. ....
11. ....
12. ....
13. ....
14. ....
15. ....
16. ....
17. ....
18. ....

"Money grows on the tree of persistence."

– Japanese Proverb

January

monday	tuesday	wednesday	thursday
1 New Year's Day	2	3	4
8	9	10	11
15 Martin Luther King Day	16	17	18
22	23	24	25
29	30	31	

2024

friday	saturday	sunday
5	6	7
12	13	14
19	20	21
26	27	28

Monthly Budget tracker

My Monthly Financial Goals

1. ....
2. ....
3. ....
4. ....
5. ....

Notes

....
....
....

Total Income	Total Expenses	Total Savings

Debts	Beginning of Month	End of Month

Home & Utilities	Budget	Spent	Personal Expenses	Budget	Spent
total			total		

January 2024

Food & Intertainment	Budget	Spent		Transportation	Budget	Spent
total				total		

Saving & Investments	Budget	Spent		Healthcare & Insurance	Budget	Spent
total				total		

Loans	Budget	Spent		Other	Budget	Spent
total				total		

Did I reach my monthly goals? Yes ☐   No ☐

February

Black History Month

monday	tuesday	wednesday	thursday
			1
5	6	7	8
12	13 *Mardi Gras*	14 *Valentine's Day*	15
19 *Presidents Day*	20	21	22
26	27	28	29

2024

friday	saturday	sunday
2 Groundhog Day	3	4
9	10	11
16	17	18
23	24	25

Monthly Budget tracker

My Monthly Financial Goals

1. ....
2. ....
3. ....
4. ....
5. ....

Notes

....
....
....

Total Income	Total Expenses	Total Savings

Debts	Beginning of Month	End of Month

Home & Utilities	Budget	Spent	Personal Expenses	Budget	Spent
total			total		

February 2024

Food & Intertainment	Budget	Spent		Transportation	Budget	Spent
total				total		

Saving & Investments	Budget	Spent		Healthcare & Insurance	Budget	Spent
total				total		

Loans	Budget	Spent		Other	Budget	Spent
total				total		

Did I reach my monthly goals?   Yes ☐   No ☐

March   Women's History Month

monday	tuesday	wednesday	thursday
4	5	6	7
11 Ramadan	12	13	14
18	19	20	21
25	26	27	28

Irish American Heritage Month 2024

friday	saturday	sunday
1	2	3
8	9	10 Daylight Saving Starts
15	16	17 St. Patrick's Day
22	23	24 Purim
29 Good Friday	30	31 Easter

Monthly Budget tracker

My Monthly Financial Goals

1. ....
2. ....
3. ....
4. ....
5. ....

Notes

....
....
....

Total Income	Total Expenses	Total Savings

Debts	Beginning of Month	End of Month

Home & Utilities	Budget	Spent		Personal Expenses	Budget	Spent
total				total		

March 2024

Food & Intertainment	Budget	Spent
total		

Transportation	Budget	Spent
total		

Saving & Investments	Budget	Spent
total		

Healthcare & Insurance	Budget	Spent
total		

Loans	Budget	Spent
total		

Other	Budget	Spent
total		

Did I reach my monthly goals?   Yes ☐   No ☐

April

monday	tuesday	wednesday	thursday
1 April Fool's Day	2	3	4
8	9	10 Eid al-Fitr	11
15	16	17	18
22 Earth Day	23 Passover	24	25
29	30		

2024

friday	saturday	sunday
5	6	7
12	13	14
19	20	21
26	27	28

....
....
....
....
....
....
....
....
....
....
....
....
....
....
....
....
....
....
....
....
....
....
....
....
....
....
....
....
....
....
....
....
....
....
....

Monthly Budget tracker

My Monthly Financial Goals

1. ....
2. ....
3. ....
4. ....
5. ....

Notes

....
....
....

Total Income	Total Expenses	Total Savings

Debts	Beginning of Month	End of Month

Home & Utilities	Budget	Spent	Personal Expenses	Budget	Spent

total   total

April 2024

Food & Intertainment	Budget	Spent
total		

Transportation	Budget	Spent
total		

Saving & Investments	Budget	Spent
total		

Healthcare & Insurance	Budget	Spent
total		

Loans	Budget	Spent
total		

Other	Budget	Spent
total		

Did I reach my monthly goals?   Yes ☐   No ☐

May

Military Appreciation Month

monday	tuesday	wednesday	thursday
		1	2
6	7	8	9
13	14	15	16
20	21	22	23
27 *Memorial Day*	28	29	30

2024

friday	saturday	sunday
3	4	5 Cinco de Mayo
10	11	12 Mother's Day
17	18 Armed Forces Day	19 Pentecost
24	25	26
31		

Monthly Budget tracker

My Monthly Financial Goals

1. ....
2. ....
3. ....
4. ....
5. ....

Notes

....
....
....

Total Income	Total Expenses	Total Savings

Debts	Beginning of Month	End of Month

Home & Utilities	Budget	Spent	Personal Expenses	Budget	Spent

total   total

May 2024

Food & Intertainment	Budget	Spent

total

Transportation	Budget	Spent

total

Saving & Investments	Budget	Spent

total

Healthcare & Insurance	Budget	Spent

total

Loans	Budget	Spent

total

Other	Budget	Spent

total

Did I reach my monthly goals? Yes ☐ No ☐

June

Pride Month

monday	tuesday	wednesday	thursday
3	4	5	6
10	11	12 Shavuot	13
17 Eid al-Adha	18	19	20
24	25	26	27

2024

friday	saturday	sunday
	1	2
7	8	9
14	15	16
Flag Day		Father's Day
21	22	23
28	29	30

Monthly Budget tracker

My Monthly Financial Goals

1. ....
2. ....
3. ....
4. ....
5. ....

Notes

....
....
....

Total Income	Total Expenses	Total Savings

Debts	Beginning of Month	End of Month

Home & Utilities	Budget	Spent	Personal Expenses	Budget	Spent
total			total		

June 2024

Food & Intertainment	Budget	Spent
total		

Transportation	Budget	Spent
total		

Saving & Investments	Budget	Spent
total		

Healthcare & Insurance	Budget	Spent
total		

Loans	Budget	Spent
total		

Other	Budget	Spent
total		

Did I reach my monthly goals? Yes ☐ No ☐

July

monday	tuesday	wednesday	thursday
1	2	3	4 Independence Day
8 Muharram	9	10	11
15	16	17	18
22	23	24	25
29	30	31	

2024

friday	saturday	sunday
5	6	7
12	13	14 Bastille Day
19	20	21
26	27	28 Parents' Day

Monthly Budget tracker

My Monthly Financial Goals

1. ....
2. ....
3. ....
4. ....
5. ....

Notes

....
....
....

Total Income	Total Expenses	Total Savings

Debts	Beginning of Month	End of Month

Home & Utilities	Budget	Spent	Personal Expenses	Budget	Spent
total			total		

July 2024

Food & Intertainment	Budget	Spent
total		

Transportation	Budget	Spent
total		

Saving & Investments	Budget	Spent
total		

Healthcare & Insurance	Budget	Spent
total		

Loans	Budget	Spent
total		

Other	Budget	Spent
total		

Did I reach my monthly goals?   Yes ☐   No ☐

August

monday	tuesday	wednesday	thursday
			1
5	6	7	8
12	13	14	15
19	20	21	22
26	27	28	29

2024

friday	saturday	sunday
2	3	4
9	10	11
16	17	18
23	24	25
30	31	

Monthly Budget tracker

My Monthly Financial Goals

1. ....
2. ....
3. ....
4. ....
5. ....

Notes

....
....
....

Total Income	Total Expenses	Total Savings

Debts	Beginning of Month	End of Month

Home & Utilities	Budget	Spent	Personal Expenses	Budget	Spent

total   total

August 2024

Food & Intertainment	Budget	Spent

total

Transportation	Budget	Spent

total

Saving & Investments	Budget	Spent

total

Healthcare & Insurance	Budget	Spent

total

Loans	Budget	Spent

total

Other	Budget	Spent

total

Did I reach my monthly goals? Yes ☐ No ☐

September

monday	tuesday	wednesday	thursday
2 Labor Day	3	4	5
9	10	11 Patriot Day	12
16 Stepfamily Day	17 Citizenship Day	18	19
23 30	24	25	26

2024

friday	saturday	sunday
		1
6	7	8 Grandparents' Day
13	14	15
20	21	22
27	28	29

Monthly Budget tracker

My Monthly Financial Goals
1. ....
2. ....
3. ....
4. ....
5. ....

Notes
....
....
....

Total Income	Total Expenses	Total Savings

Debts	Beginning of Month	End of Month

Home & Utilities	Budget	Spent	Personal Expenses	Budget	Spent
total			total		

September 2024

Food & Intertainment	Budget	Spent
total		

Transportation	Budget	Spent
total		

Saving & Investments	Budget	Spent
total		

Healthcare & Insurance	Budget	Spent
total		

Loans	Budget	Spent
total		

Other	Budget	Spent
total		

Did I reach my monthly goals? Yes ☐ No ☐

October

monday	tuesday	wednesday	thursday
	1	2	3 Rosh Hashana
7	8	9	10
14 Columbus Day	15	16	17 Sukkot
21	22	23	24
28	29	30	31 Halloween

2024

friday	saturday	sunday
4	5	6
11	12 Yom Kippur	13
18	19	20
25	26	27

Monthly Budget tracker

My Monthly Financial Goals

1. ....
2. ....
3. ....
4. ....
5. ....

Notes

....
....
....

Total Income	Total Expenses	Total Savings

Debts	Beginning of Month	End of Month

Home & Utilities	Budget	Spent	Personal Expenses	Budget	Spent
total			total		

October 2024

Food & Intertainment	Budget	Spent		Transportation	Budget	Spent
total				total		

Saving & Investments	Budget	Spent		Healthcare & Insurance	Budget	Spent
total				total		

Loans	Budget	Spent		Other	Budget	Spent
total				total		

Did I reach my monthly goals?   Yes ☐   No ☐

November

monday	tuesday	wednesday	thursday
4	5	6	7
11 Veterans' Day	12	13	14
18	19	20	21
25	26	27	28 Thanksgiving

2024

friday	saturday	sunday
1	2	3 Daylight Saving Ends
8	9	10
15	16	17
22	23	24
29 Black Friday	30	

Monthly Budget tracker

My Monthly Financial Goals

1. ....
2. ....
3. ....
4. ....
5. ....

Notes

....
....
....

Total Income	Total Expenses	Total Savings

Debts	Beginning of Month	End of Month

Home & Utilities	Budget	Spent	Personal Expenses	Budget	Spent

total   total

November 2024

Food & Intertainment	Budget	Spent		Transportation	Budget	Spent
total				total		

Saving & Investments	Budget	Spent		Healthcare & Insurance	Budget	Spent
total				total		

Loans	Budget	Spent		Other	Budget	Spent
total				total		

Did I reach my monthly goals?   Yes ☐   No ☐

December

monday	tuesday	wednesday	thursday
2 Cyber Monday	3	4	5
9	10	11	12
16	17	18	19
23	24 Christmas Eve	25 Christmas Day	26 Hanukkah
30	31 New Year's Eve		

2024

friday	saturday	sunday
		1
6	7 Pearl Harbor Remembrance Day	8
13	14	15
20	21	22
27	28	29

Monthly Budget tracker

My Monthly Financial Goals

1. ....
2. ....
3. ....
4. ....
5. ....

Notes

....
....
....

Total Income	Total Expenses	Total Savings

Debts	Beginning of Month	End of Month

Home & Utilities	Budget	Spent	Personal Expenses	Budget	Spent
total			total		

December 2024

Food & Intertainment	Budget	Spent
total		

Transportation	Budget	Spent
total		

Saving & Investments	Budget	Spent
total		

Healthcare & Insurance	Budget	Spent
total		

Loans	Budget	Spent
total		

Other	Budget	Spent
total		

Did I reach my monthly goals?   Yes ☐   No ☐

My 2025 Resolutions

1 ....
2 ....
3 ....
4 ....
5 ....
6 ....
7 ....
8 ....
9 ....
10 ....
11 ....
12 ....
13 ....
14 ....
15 ....
16 ....
17 ....
18 ....

"Wealth is the ability to fully experience life."

— Henry David Thoreau

January

monday	tuesday	wednesday	thursday
		1 New Year's Day	2
6	7	8	9
13	14	15	16
20 Martin Luther King Day	21	22	23
27	28	29	30

2025

friday	saturday	sunday
3	4	5
10	11	12
17	18	19
24	25	26
31		

Monthly Budget tracker

My Monthly Financial Goals

1. ....
2. ....
3. ....
4. ....
5. ....

Notes

....
....
....

Total Income	Total Expenses	Total Savings

Debts	Beginning of Month	End of Month

Home & Utilities	Budget	Spent	Personal Expenses	Budget	Spent
total			total		

January 2025

Food & Intertainment	Budget	Spent
total		

Transportation	Budget	Spent
total		

Saving & Investments	Budget	Spent
total		

Healthcare & Insurance	Budget	Spent
total		

Loans	Budget	Spent
total		

Other	Budget	Spent
total		

Did I reach my monthly goals?   Yes ☐   No ☐

February

Black History Month

monday	tuesday	wednesday	thursday
3	4	5	6
10	11	12	13
17 Presidents Day	18	19	20
24	25	26	27

2025

friday	saturday	sunday
	1	2 Groundhog Day
7	8	9
14 Valentine's Day	15	16
21	22	23
28		

Monthly Budget tracker

My Monthly Financial Goals

1. ....
2. ....
3. ....
4. ....
5. ....

Notes

....
....
....

Total Income	Total Expenses	Total Savings

Debts	Beginning of Month	End of Month

Home & Utilities	Budget	Spent	Personal Expenses	Budget	Spent
total			total		

February 2025

Food & Intertainment	Budget	Spent

total

Transportation	Budget	Spent

total

Saving & Investments	Budget	Spent

total

Healthcare & Insurance	Budget	Spent

total

Loans	Budget	Spent

total

Other	Budget	Spent

total

Did I reach my monthly goals?   Yes ☐   No ☐

March

Women's History Month

monday	tuesday	wednesday	thursday
3	4	5	6
	Mardi Gras		
10	11	12	13
17	18	19	20
St. Patrick's Day			
24	25	26	27
31			
Eid al-Fitr			

Irish American Heritage Month 2025

friday	saturday	sunday
	1	2
	Ramadan	
7	8	9
		Daylight Saving Starts
14	15	16
Purim		
21	22	23
28	29	30

Monthly Budget tracker

My Monthly Financial Goals

1. ....
2. ....
3. ....
4. ....
5. ....

Notes

....
....
....

Total Income	Total Expenses	Total Savings

Debts	Beginning of Month	End of Month

Home & Utilities	Budget	Spent	Personal Expenses	Budget	Spent
total			total		

March 2025

Food & Intertainment	Budget	Spent

total

Transportation	Budget	Spent

total

Saving & Investments	Budget	Spent

total

Healthcare & Insurance	Budget	Spent

total

Loans	Budget	Spent

total

Other	Budget	Spent

total

Did I reach my monthly goals?   Yes ☐   No ☐

April

monday	tuesday	wednesday	thursday
	1 April Fool's Day	2	3
7	8	9	10
14	15	16	17
21	22 Earth Day	23	24
28	29	30	

2025

friday	saturday	sunday
4	5	6
11	12	13 Passover
18 Good Friday	19	20 Easter
25	26	27

Monthly Budget tracker

My Monthly Financial Goals

1. ....
2. ....
3. ....
4. ....
5. ....

Notes

....
....
....

Total Income	Total Expenses	Total Savings

Debts	Beginning of Month	End of Month

Home & Utilities	Budget	Spent	Personal Expenses	Budget	Spent
total			total		

April 2025

Food & Intertainment	Budget	Spent
total		

Transportation	Budget	Spent
total		

Saving & Investments	Budget	Spent
total		

Healthcare & Insurance	Budget	Spent
total		

Loans	Budget	Spent
total		

Other	Budget	Spent
total		

Did I reach my monthly goals?   Yes ☐   No ☐

May

Military Appreciation Month

monday	tuesday	wednesday	thursday
			1
5 Cinco de Mayo	6	7	8
12	13	14	15
19	20	21	22
26 Memorial Day	27	28	29

2025

friday	saturday	sunday
2	3	4
9	10	11 Mother's Day
16	17 Armed Forces Day	18
23	24	25
30	31	

Monthly Budget tracker

My Monthly Financial Goals

1. ....
2. ....
3. ....
4. ....
5. ....

Notes

....
....
....

Total Income	Total Expenses	Total Savings

Debts	Beginning of Month	End of Month

Home & Utilities	Budget	Spent	Personal Expenses	Budget	Spent

total   total

May 2025

Food & Intertainment	Budget	Spent
total		

Transportation	Budget	Spent
total		

Saving & Investments	Budget	Spent
total		

Healthcare & Insurance	Budget	Spent
total		

Loans	Budget	Spent
total		

Other	Budget	Spent
total		

Did I reach my monthly goals? Yes ☐ No ☐

June

Pride Month

monday	tuesday	wednesday	thursday
2 Shavuot	3	4	5
9	10	11	12
16	17	18	19
23 / 30	24	25	26

2025

friday	saturday	sunday
		1
6	7	8
	Eid al-Adha	Pentecost
13	14	15
	Flag Day	Father's Day
20	21	22
27	28	29
Muharram		

Monthly Budget tracker

My Monthly Financial Goals

1. ....
2. ....
3. ....
4. ....
5. ....

Notes

....
....
....

Total Income	Total Expenses	Total Savings

Debts	Beginning of Month	End of Month

Home & Utilities	Budget	Spent	Personal Expenses	Budget	Spent

total   total

June 2025

Food & Intertainment	Budget	Spent
total		

Transportation	Budget	Spent
total		

Saving & Investments	Budget	Spent
total		

Healthcare & Insurance	Budget	Spent
total		

Loans	Budget	Spent
total		

Other	Budget	Spent
total		

Did I reach my monthly goals?   Yes ☐   No ☐

July

monday	tuesday	wednesday	thursday
	1	2	3
7	8	9	10
14 Bastille Day	15	16	17
21	22	23	24
28	29	30	31

2025

friday	saturday	sunday
4	5	6
11	12	13
18	19	20
25	26	27 Parents' Day

Monthly Budget tracker

My Monthly Financial Goals

1. ....
2. ....
3. ....
4. ....
5. ....

Notes

....
....
....

Total Income	Total Expenses	Total Savings

Debts	Beginning of Month	End of Month

Home & Utilities	Budget	Spent	Personal Expenses	Budget	Spent
total			total		

July 2025

Food & Intertainment	Budget	Spent
total		

Transportation	Budget	Spent
total		

Saving & Investments	Budget	Spent
total		

Healthcare & Insurance	Budget	Spent
total		

Loans	Budget	Spent
total		

Other	Budget	Spent
total		

Did I reach my monthly goals?   Yes ☐   No ☐

August

monday	tuesday	wednesday	thursday
4	5	6	7
11	12	13	14
18	19	20	21
25	26	27	28

2025

friday	saturday	sunday
1	2	3
8	9	10
15	16	17
22	23	24
29	30	31

Monthly Budget tracker

My Monthly Financial Goals
1. ....
2. ....
3. ....
4. ....
5. ....

Notes
....
....
....

Total Income	Total Expenses	Total Savings

Debts	Beginning of Month	End of Month

Home & Utilities	Budget	Spent	Personal Expenses	Budget	Spent
total			total		

August 2025

Food & Intertainment	Budget	Spent		Transportation	Budget	Spent
total				**total**		

Saving & Investments	Budget	Spent		Healthcare & Insurance	Budget	Spent
total				**total**		

Loans	Budget	Spent		Other	Budget	Spent
total				**total**		

Did I reach my monthly goals? Yes ☐ No ☐

September

monday	tuesday	wednesday	thursday
1 Labor Day	2	3	4
8	9	10	11 Patriot Day
15	16 Stepfamily Day	17 Citizenship Day	18
22	23 Rosh Hashana	24	25
29	30		

2025

friday	saturday	sunday
5	6	7 Grandparents' Day
12	13	14
19	20	21
26	27	28

Monthly Budget tracker

My Monthly Financial Goals

1. ....
2. ....
3. ....
4. ....
5. ....

Notes

....
....
....

Total Income	Total Expenses	Total Savings

Debts	Beginning of Month	End of Month

Home & Utilities	Budget	Spent	Personal Expenses	Budget	Spent
total			total		

September 2025

Food & Intertainment	Budget	Spent
total		

Transportation	Budget	Spent
total		

Saving & Investments	Budget	Spent
total		

Healthcare & Insurance	Budget	Spent
total		

Loans	Budget	Spent
total		

Other	Budget	Spent
total		

Did I reach my monthly goals?   Yes ☐   No ☐

October

monday	tuesday	wednesday	thursday
		1	2 Yom Kippur
6	7 Sukkot	8	9
13 Columbus Day	14	15	16
20	21	22	23
27	28	29	30

2025

friday	saturday	sunday
3	4	5
10	11	12
17	18	19
24	25	26
31 Halloween		

Monthly Budget tracker

My Monthly Financial Goals

1. ....
2. ....
3. ....
4. ....
5. ....

Notes

....
....
....

Total Income	Total Expenses	Total Savings

Debts	Beginning of Month	End of Month

Home & Utilities	Budget	Spent	Personal Expenses	Budget	Spent
total			total		

October 2025

Food & Intertainment	Budget	Spent		Transportation	Budget	Spent
total				total		

Saving & Investments	Budget	Spent		Healthcare & Insurance	Budget	Spent
total				total		

Loans	Budget	Spent		Other	Budget	Spent
total				total		

Did I reach my monthly goals?   Yes ☐   No ☐

November

monday	tuesday	wednesday	thursday
3	4	5	6
10	11 Veterans' Day	12	13
17	18	19	20
24	25	26	27 Thanksgiving

2025

friday	saturday	sunday
	1	2 Daylight Saving Ends
7	8	9
14	15	16
21	22	23
28 Black Friday	29	30

Monthly Budget tracker

My Monthly Financial Goals

1. ....
2. ....
3. ....
4. ....
5. ....

Notes

....
....
....

Total Income	Total Expenses	Total Savings

Debts	Beginning of Month	End of Month

Home & Utilities	Budget	Spent	Personal Expenses	Budget	Spent
total			total		

November 2025

Food & Intertainment	Budget	Spent		Transportation	Budget	Spent
total				total		

Saving & Investments	Budget	Spent		Healthcare & Insurance	Budget	Spent
total				total		

Loans	Budget	Spent		Other	Budget	Spent
total				total		

Did I reach my monthly goals?   Yes ☐   No ☐

December

monday	tuesday	wednesday	thursday
1 Cyber Monday	2	3	4
8	9	10	11
15 Hanukkah	16	17	18
22	23	24 Christmas Eve	25 Christmas Day
29	30	31 New Year's Eve	

2025

friday	saturday	sunday
5	6	7 Pearl Harbor Remembrance Day
12	13	14
19	20	21
26	27	28

Monthly Budget tracker

My Monthly Financial Goals

1. ....
2. ....
3. ....
4. ....
5. ....

Notes

....
....
....

Total Income	Total Expenses	Total Savings

Debts	Beginning of Month	End of Month

Home & Utilities	Budget	Spent	Personal Expenses	Budget	Spent

total   total

December 2025

Food & Intertainment	Budget	Spent
total		

Transportation	Budget	Spent
total		

Saving & Investments	Budget	Spent
total		

Healthcare & Insurance	Budget	Spent
total		

Loans	Budget	Spent
total		

Other	Budget	Spent
total		

Did I reach my monthly goals?   Yes ☐   No ☐

www.ingramcontent.com/pod-product-compliance
Lightning Source LLC
LaVergne TN
LVHW020425070526
838199LV00003B/280